SHE.

TO THE REBIRTH OF HER SOUL

FAISEENA FAISAL

To my mother, Ramla, who once said, *"You carry your father's name, but mine is unheard."*

This book is my way of writing your name into the world, of letting it echo in the hearts of those who read these words. You are the first poem I ever knew; the strength in my roots, the warmth in my journey, the quiet force that has shaped me into who I am.

May your name be remembered, always.

Contents

Contents

Preface

"she" is not just a collection of poems; it is a journey one that began long ago, in different moments, at different stages of my life. These poems were not written in a single sitting, nor do they belong to a single time. They are pieces of emotions, fragments of stories; some mine, some of the women around me, and some that were whispered in passing but stayed in my heart.

I began writing these poems whenever I encountered a woman's unspoken pain, quiet strength, or untold story. Each poem carries the echoes of voices that were never raised, the weight of emotions that were never expressed, and the silent resilience of women who endured, loved, and fought their battles in silence. I wanted this book to be a voice for those who feel unheard and to capture the essence of womanhood in all its forms.

Now that I have completed this book in my postpartum period while balancing my career, I see it as more than just a collection of poetry; its a reflection of my own evolution as a woman. Just like these words, I have grown, changed, and carried countless experiences with me. And in these pages, I hope every woman finds a piece of herself; a reminder that she is seen, heard, and she is never alone. So this is for you...

With love,

Faiceena Faisal

1. the one who healed her

nestled deep in warmth and dark,
a flicker of life, a beating spark.
i hear the whispers, soft yet near,
murmurs drifting, faint but clear.
"*a boy,*" he says, with hopeful tone,
"*a son to call his very own.*
but if it's a girl… well, i wouldn't despair."
mama smiles, a tight-lipped grace,
"*yeah, me too,*" in this still space.
her breath is shallow, her hands so cold,
i feel her worries, deep and old.
at least, i think, she will be glad,
but then i sense the thoughts she had—
"*what if it's a girl again?*"
her fear, her guilt… it starts to rain.
why am i not the dream you see?
do i not have the right to be?
to breathe, to laugh, to simply be?
"*forgive me, child, i wished for a son,*
what kind of mother have i become?"
"*forgive me, child,*" her tears may fall,
"*i know the pain, i've felt it all.*"
she held me close, fierce and true,
and though i came unwanted first,
i was the one who healed her worst.

2. a father's pride

come, my child, sit with me.
let me say what i should have said long ago.
for years, i carried a belief so deep,
never realizing it was wrong, never letting it go.
i never spoke about it, but in my heart, i always knew,
that while i loved you, i also held you back;
if only i had seen it through.
i always wished for a son;
not because i didn't love you,
but because that's what i was told,
that a son is strength, a son is pride,
but a daughter is a burden to hold.
my father once told me, "*a daughter is a responsibility,*
a debt you must repay,
raise her well, protect her always,
but don't let her fly away."
and so, i did what i thought was right;
kept you safe, i kept you near,
but in doing that, i also held you back,
wrapped you in my fear.
you wanted to run, to dream, to fly,
but i was afraid of what lay ahead,
so i pulled you down, i clipped your wings,
i let my worries fill your head.
not once did i ask, "*what does she want?*"

not once did i say, *"go on, try,"*
instead, i warned you, *"stay on the ground,"*
while you longed to touch the sky.
and yet, despite me, despite the weight,
you found your way, you broke free,
you built your own path, you climbed those walls,
and became what you were meant to be.
and now, i stand here, watching you shine,
standing taller than i ever dreamed,
my daughter, my pride, my deepest regret;
how blind i had been.
i thought i was protecting you,
keeping you safe from a world so tough,
but in doing so, i became the first cage,
and that was more than enough.
yet, even when i held you back,
you never let go of your fire inside,
you rose, you soared, and now,
i must lift my head to meet your eyes.
and i, who once thought i knew best,
now realize how wrong i was,
for i did not make you strong;
you were strong all along, despite my cause.
forgive me, my child, if you can,
for the dreams i dimmed, the years i stole,
for all the times i pulled you down,
out of fear, out of control.
i see now that a daughter isn't a weight,

a worry, a burden to bear,

she is light, she is fire, she is a storm;

fierce, fearless, rare.

you were never my duty, never a debt,

never something to confine,

you were always my greatest blessing,

my reason to feel pride.

and if i could turn back time,

if i could change just one thing,

i wouldn't hold you down;

i would hold your wings.

but here you are, despite it all,

standing where i never let you go,

and here i am, an old man now,

watching all that you have shown.

if i failed, then let my failure be that,

i didn't see this before today, that a daughter, too,

can be a father's greatest pride in every single way.

so go, my child, without fear, without doubt, without regret,

know that now, as i watch you rise,

my heart is filled with love, not debt.

not in guilt, not in pain,

but in awe, in joy, in pride,

for my daughter, you have made this father the proudest one alive.

3. it's a baby girl

a tiny soul arrives tonight,
wrapped in warmth, bathed in soft light.
little fingers curl, a heart so new,
but even before she takes her first breath,
the whispers begin.
her father stands quietly, his face unreadable,
while the room hums with hushed laughter and knowing looks.
advice pours in like a never-ending tide—
"start saving now. forget the luxuries."
"oh… another girl? so sad.
your husband must have wanted a son."
no one stops to see the tiny miracle before them.
she's only hours old, yet already judged.
some try to offer comfort, their words empty and rehearsed—
"daughters are a hidden blessing."
"a guaranteed path to heaven."
but why does love, when explained,
feel more like an apology?
and yet, in the midst of it all, there is one light—
my mother's arms, her unwavering smile.
she doesn't see a burden, a responsibility, or a regret.
she sees her dream come true.
to her, i'm not just a daughter.
i am a piece of her heart, a love beyond measure.
and in that embrace, i know—

i am wanted. i am cherished.
i am loved, fiercely, forever.

4. my forever friend

people always said we looked alike—they couldn't tell us apart.
seven years between us, but to them, we were one and the same.
we'd just laugh, shaking our heads,
because they didn't see what we did—
that time never mattered. you were always a part of me.
side by side, we took on the world, hand in hand.
i was your safe place, and you were my light.
when life felt too heavy, you stood strong for me,
and when you stumbled, i was there to steady you.
scraped knees, broken hearts, endless late-night talks—
you never judged, just listened.
you held my hand when i was too scared to try,
and i wiped your tears when the world let you down.
we're different in so many ways—
you, the sun. me, the rain.
yet somehow, we just make sense.
two halves of the same whole,
woven together by blood and something even deeper.
we fought, we hurt, but we never broke.
like waves crashing hard, yet always finding their way back to shore.
and if i had to choose a sister, in this life or the next,
i'd choose you. every time.

5. she came for me

they said having a daughter would be payback—
as if love had a way of circling back to punish,
as if my past would find its way to me
through the tiny hands of a girl who carried my name.
but they were wrong.
she is not my reckoning—she is my gift.
not a lesson i had to learn, but a love i finally got to receive.
a softness i thought i'd lost, placed gently back into my hands.
she is not the echo of my mistakes—
she is the redemption i never believed i deserved.
she did not come to wound me; she came to heal.
she presses her cheek against mine,
small fingers tracing the lines of my face,
whispering, mom, you're so pretty.
and in that moment, i see myself through her eyes.
she doesn't search for the cracks, the scars,
or the past i tried so hard to outrun.
she only sees me—
the mother who stays,
the arms that hold her close,
the voice that soothes her back to sleep.
she is the love i once gave freely
but never had returned.
the laughter i longed for in my childhood home,
the warmth i searched for in all the wrong places.

she is a second chance at childhood—
not mine, but hers.
untouched by the pain i once knew.
i watch her run barefoot through the grass,
hair wild, eyes bright,
and i think—this is what freedom looks like.
she does not carry my trauma—
she sees the world unburdened by it.
they said she would be my payback.
but she is my redemption.
she has softened the edges i sharpened to survive,
made me gentle in ways i never knew i could be.
she has given me the love i once begged for—
without hesitation, without conditions.
she has taught me that love does not abandon,
does not have to be earned.
that real love stays.
and so, i built a world where i could both mother and create,
a space where my voice could be heard,
where my words could hold others the way i hold her.
i write about her, about us,
about the way motherhood became my rebirth.
a mother needs a daughter,
not just to cradle in her arms,
but to teach her what love without conditions looks like.
and when i look at her, i know—deep in my bones—
she is the soulmate i spent a lifetime searching for.
there she stands,
fearless, brilliant, radiant,

teaching me more about love
than i ever thought possible.
she has shown me that love is not sacrifice,
not shrinking, not losing yourself to be chosen—
but standing tall, taking up space,
knowing you are worthy simply because you are.
and as i watch her spin in the golden light,
singing at the top of her lungs,
arms reaching for the sky,
i know—
she didn't just come from me.
she came for me.

6. the truth about being a girl

girlhood was never about hating dresses,
but the way they were given to us—
soft fabric wrapped in heavy rules,
stitched with expectations we never chose.
we never hated cooking,
but the whispers that came with it—
"what will happen after she gets married?"
as if our worth was measured
in folded dough and perfect spices.
we never despised household chores,
but the weight of being told—
"a good girl must know these things."
not for survival, not for joy,
but to fit a mold we never asked for.
they taught us these things,
not for ourselves, not for independence,
but to build a home
that would never truly be ours.
they showed us how to please, how to sacrifice—
but never how to ask, how to say no.
they taught us patience, but never freedom.
they taught us silence, but never how to take up space.
and so, without knowing why, we rebelled—
not against the chores, not against the skills,
but against the cage built around them.

and so, we ran.
at first, barefoot on warm earth,
racing the wind, laughing, free.
no one told us to slow down.
no one asked us to be less.
then, the rules changed.
they told us to shrink, to soften,
to be delicate, to be less.
we were too loud, too wild,
our voices carried too far,
our ambitions stretched too wide.
they placed ceilings above our heads,
chains around our ankles,
limits on our dreams.
and so, we ran again.
this time, not for fun,
but for space, for freedom,
for the right to move, to choose,
to exist without apology.
"run like a girl."
now, it means breaking through barriers,
pushing past voices that say we can't,
defying rules that were never meant to protect us—
only to contain us.
have you seen a woman run for her life?
she does not run like a whisper, but like a storm.
she runs as if fire burns behind her,
as if the ground itself dares to hold her back.
she runs through the thick air of every *"no"*

she was ever told—

as if her heart knows that stopping means surrender.

she does not stop.

she does not look back.

because little girls grow.

and when they do,

they become unstoppable women.

7. the eldest daughter

she grew up fast, without a choice,
a quiet heart, a steady voice.
a daughter, a sister, a second mom,
always strong, always calm.
"you don't care," they often said,
"you never feel—you don't get upset."
but she did—oh, she felt so much,
she just never learned to show it enough.
she cared for her mother, frail with time,
held her hand in the cold midnight.
she saw her father, weary and worn,
he hid his storm, but she felt the storm.
yet how to show it? she wasn't sure.
"just because i carry it well," she'd think,
"doesn't mean it's not heavy," she'd blink.
her heart was young, yet burdened deep,
too many promises, too much to keep.
she loved them all but craved her space,
a single word could leave a trace.
she built up walls, she trusted few,
but love still lived within her, too.
she solved their problems, dried their tears,
yet no one saw her hidden fears.
she had no refuge, no safe place,
she carried it all—alone, with grace.

"*you're so mature,*" they'd always say,
"*you never break, you'll be okay.*"
but did they see the weight she bore?
did they ask if she could take much more?
"*i'm the eldest daughter,*" she'd sigh,
"a soldier drafted by the sky."
shielding siblings, taking the fall,
standing strong through it all.
she gave them all she never had,
held their hands, ignored her sad.
not asking for pity, nor seeking praise,
just longing for lighter days.
to the eldest daughters, quiet and tough,
i see you—i know it's rough.
but please, don't forget your heart,
love yourself, too—let that be the start.

8. the things i wish you knew

have you ever gripped your keys so tight
they left marks in your palm—
not because you might lose them,
but because they felt like the only weapon you had?
have you ever called for a ride,
even when home was just a few steps away,
because you felt eyes crawling on your skin,
footsteps echoing a little too close behind?
do you pick your shoes based on how fast you can run?
not for comfort, not for style—
but because she might have to run?
not a jog, not a sprint for sport,
but a run-for-your-life kind of run,
a run no one should ever have to plan for.
have you ever shared your location,
not for fun, not for plans,
but just in case you disappear?
have you ever whispered to yourself,
"if something happens, at least they'll know where to start looking?"
the world has made her believe
she is never truly safe—
not in the streets, not in her home,
not even in her own skin.
have you ever closed the curtains,
not for privacy, not to block out the sun,

but because you felt eyes where there should be none?
because you swore you saw a shadow shift,
because you know that glass is never truly a wall?
have you ever walked alone at night,
headphones tucked away in your pocket,
because she needs to listen—
for footsteps, for whispers, for danger breathing too close?
because music is a luxury
when survival demands attention.
do you know how hard it is for her to just exist?
to breathe without fear clawing at her throat?
to take up space without feeling like prey?
to dress without questioning
what message her clothes might send—
to those who believe that no is negotiable,
that silence is consent,
that her body is not her own?
have you ever felt like your body wasn't yours,
like a stranger's touch burned long after they walked away,
like a smile from the wrong person
was a warning, not a kindness?
do you know what it's like to live like this?
to survive when all you want is to live?
because i do.
every day, i do.
she's tired—so, so tired.
of walking fast but not too fast.
of looking over her shoulder.
of carrying fear like a second skin.

and yet, she survives.
every day, she survives.
but survival is not living.
it never was.
it's time we change that.

9. what i gave away

there was a time when i woke up without aching,

without a tiny voice calling my name before the sun had even risen.

there was a time when my body was just mine,

when my hands only cared for myself,

when my reflection showed a girl who had time—

time to rest, time to dream, time to be.

i used to stand in front of the mirror,

turning side to side, checking my hair,

frowning at my waist,

sighing at the way my body curved,

wishing i could change a little here, a little there.

i thought i wasn't good enough.

i thought i had flaws.

i didn't know—

that was the best i would ever look,

the best i would ever feel.

and then, i carried life inside me,

felt the stretch of skin, the weight of existence,

felt my bones shift to make space for someone else.

i watched my body become a home,

watched it give and give,

until there was nothing left that belonged to just me.

and as i pushed life into this world,

i felt something leave me.

it wasn't just the pain,

it wasn't just the child—
it was the girl i used to be.
now, i wake up to a different version of myself,
eyes heavy with exhaustion,
hair tangled in yesterday's neglect,
a body that no longer fits the clothes of my past.
i do not recognize the woman in the mirror,
but she stares back at me,
holding the weight of love and sacrifice
in the circles beneath her eyes.
and then, he asks me—
"what happened to the girl i married?"
he doesn't see that she is gone,
he looks for her in my tired face,
he does not understand—
she did not just disappear,
she died.
she didn't mean to fade,
but she gave too much of herself away,
and there was nothing left for her.
and yet, in her place stands something greater,
a mother who gives without asking,
who holds tiny hands instead of dreams,
who no longer belongs to herself,
but to the child who calls her name.
i may never be carefree again,
never be the same girl who once twirled in front of mirrors,
but i have become a world,
a home,

a love that never fades.
because when i look down,
and i see the little hands reaching for me,
the little voice calling me mama,
i know that i may have lost myself—
but i have found something greater.
i am not the girl i once was.
i am a mother.

10. the heart that heals

i asked my mother, "*if you're not here, whom should i call?*"
she smiled and whispered, "*your aunt, my child, she will answer them all.*"
"she is the only soul i trust in this world so wide,
she loves you as i do, with arms open wide.
the only selfless heart that beats for you,
no matter the hour, no matter what you do."
"if she hears you're in trouble, no matter how far,
she'll run to you, like a shooting star.
with all her might, without a doubt,
she'll fight the world to pull you out."
"she once told me, '*with my whole life, i will love,
i will stand with them when push comes to shove.*'
and isn't it true, my dear little one?
so call her, my child, when my time is done."
they say an aunt is a second mother's grace,
a special bond time cannot erase.
at times, her strength surpasses mine,
a love that's truly divine.
no one can replace her, not even a mom,
for she will move heaven and earth till the storms are gone.
"that's why i say, call her, my dear,
she'll be your shelter when i'm not near.
call her, my child, when i'm not near,
for in her embrace, you will find me here."

11. for the woman who gave everything

how do i tell you, mom,
that your arms were the home i longed for,
the only place where the world felt quiet,
where i could rest without fear?
nothing will ever match the warmth
of your tired hands brushing my hair back,
or the quiet strength in your voice
when the world felt too heavy for me to carry.
i get my hustle from you—
from the woman who never stopped,
not when she was exhausted,
not when life tested her in ways she never deserved.
i watched you push forward
with a fire that never burned out,
even when i knew you were running on empty.
and now, i carry that fire within me,
because i never saw you quit.
not once.
but, mom, i saw what it cost you—
every late night, every silent sigh,
every dream placed on a high shelf…
where they grew dusty and out of reach.
i saw the way you had convinced yourself
that what you wanted no longer mattered—

that your dreams were a luxury

you couldn't afford to have

because you had children who needed you more.

you gave up the life you wanted,

so i could have the one you never got to live.

i wish i could have told you back then—

you deserved to choose yourself too.

i have watched you stay strong,

not because you chose to,

but because you believed you had no choice.

i have seen you bite your tongue

when you wanted to cry,

force a smile when the world was unkind,

swallow your pain

as if it were something you weren't allowed to feel.

and i wish i could go back

and hold the girl you were before you were my mother,

before the weight of responsibility

pushed you to the side of your own life.

sometimes, in my dreams,

i see you in another world.

a world where you wake up and breathe,

without a list of worries waiting for you.

a world where the dishes stay in the sink,

where you dance in the kitchen

without looking over your shoulder,

and in that world, mom—

you are whole.

not because of anyone,

but because you finally chose you.
i pray to god every day—
not for riches, not for success—
but for time.
time to give you back
even a fraction of what you gave me.
time to tell you that everything i am,
everything i have,
is because of you.
time to show you that your sacrifices weren't in vain,
that your love shaped a life you can be proud of.
"because behind every story,
there's a mother's untold story—
the one that made mine possible."
if they ask me what my greatest blessing is,
i will say, without hesitation—
my mother's voice at home.
the sound of comfort,
the sound of safety,
the sound of love in its purest form.
the sound i never want to live without.
and i'm sorry, mom.
i realize too late that you are not just my mother.
you are a girl too.
a girl who never had all the answers,
who was also living this life for the first time,
figuring it out as she went.
and if i could,
i would give up my own existence

just to see you happy,
just to see you finally rest,
just to see you become the woman
you once dreamed of being.
because you deserve that too.

12. to my first child

dear Nemo,
they told me time would fly, but i never really believed them—
not until i blinked, and the tiny girl with chubby cheeks
and wide, wondering eyes was gone.
not until the little hands that once clung to mine
grew steady, strong, capable of holding their own.
not until the voice that once called my name
in giggles and endless questions
became the voice that calms me now,
the voice that tells me, i'm here.
how fast you grew, little one.
one moment, you were tripping over your own feet,
trying to match my steps,
copying every little thing i did—
wearing my clothes, my lipstick, my laughter.
you just wanted to be near me,
to be like me,
and god, how i wish i had known then
how much i would one day long for those days back.
i look at our old pictures,
and something tightens in my chest.
there you are—so small, so innocent,
so unaware of how time would pull us forward,
how quickly childhood fades.
a child who only wanted to belong at my side.

i used to roll my eyes when you begged to sleep next to me,
but the night you finally stopped asking,
i stared at the empty space beside me
and missed you more than i ever thought possible.
you were my first lesson in love, nemo,
the first child i ever learned to care for.
before i was a mother, i was your sister—
your second mom without ever meaning to be.
and now, i watch as you hold my babies,
the same way i once held you,
rocking them with that same tenderness
that once rested in my arms.
how strange it is—
the girl who once reached for my hand
now stands beside me, not as my shadow,
but as my equal, as my anchor.
and oh, how i regret the moments i pushed you away,
the seconds i let slip through my fingers.
i didn't know, nemo.
i didn't know you would grow up so fast.
i didn't know there would come a day
when you would wipe my tears instead of me wiping yours.
that your hugs would become my safe place.
that your laughter would become my comfort.
hugs, hand-holding, and no more blackmail?
are we even the same sisters?
no, we are something more now.
time has carved us into something unshakable,
something deeper than childhood rivalry,

something stronger than blood.
so i write this for you, my dear first child—
for the girl who shaped me into the woman i am.
so that when you doubt yourself,
when the world tries to make you feel small,
you will remember who you are.
you were that sweet, stubborn, messy-haired girl
who wanted nothing more than to be like me.
and now, i look at you,
and all i want is for you to be exactly who you are.
and i hope—more than anything—
that life gives you everything you dream of,
that love finds you,
that joy wraps itself around you and never lets go.
but even if the world is unkind,
even if life feels too heavy,
know that i will always be here,
cheering for you, fighting for you,
just as i did when you were that little girl
who just wanted to be like me.
i can't imagine a life without you, nemo.
not then.
not now.
not ever.
with all my love,
your big sister.

13. whole on my own

they tell you to marry,
to have kids, to settle down,
as if love is the only home worth building,
as if your worth is measured
by the weight of a ring on your finger.
but i see you—
the strong, unshaken woman in the back of my mind,
the one who refuses to shrink,
who knows that, before belonging to anyone,
she must first belong to herself.
settle down, they say.
but settle down for yourself first—
settle your heart, your dreams, your ambitions.
do not rush to place your happiness
into hands that may not know how to hold it.
build your world, brick by brick,
with your own name written on the walls,
with a door that no one else holds the key to.
take your financial life seriously—
not as an option, but as a necessity.
make money, make more than enough,
because the world is not kind to poor women.
because independence is not just about freedom,
it is about survival, about dignity,
about never having to stay where you are not cherished,

about walking away with your head held high.

and when you love, love with a full heart—

but never at the cost of your own voice.

you should never have to ask a man for something twice.

if you do, he has already decided you are not a priority.

and that is your answer,

as loud as silence, as clear as a closed door.

hold yourself to this truth—

you deserve to be heard the first time.

you deserve the kind of love that listens,

that remembers, that shows up.

so, be the woman who stands tall,

who owns her choices, her body, her future.

do not let them rush you into their timelines,

into a love that cages instead of frees.

be the woman who knows that marriage is not an escape,

that children are not a duty,

that a life well-lived is not defined by

who stands beside you,

but by how boldly you walk alone.

and if love comes, let it be a blessing, not a rescue.

let it be an addition, never the foundation.

because you, my dear, are already whole.

14. lost in silence

i spent so much of my life in silence,
walking through days with my head down,
hustling, grinding, pushing forward,
never stopping to ask myself if this was the life i wanted.
i told myself that hard work would make it all worth it,
that if i just kept going, one day, i would feel whole.
but somewhere along the way, i lost myself.
i forgot the sound of my own voice,
forgot the dreams i once held so close to my heart.
i became so good at staying quiet,
so good at not taking up space,
that i started to disappear.
and then, one day, i looked up.
i looked around at the life i had built,
the things i had sacrificed for,
the sleepless nights, the endless worrying,
and i realized—none of it really mattered.
the things i had poured my heart into,
they never truly loved me back.
they were just empty pursuits,
disguised as purpose,
wrapped in expectations i never questioned.
i spent years being afraid to speak,
afraid to take up space,
afraid that my voice wasn't enough.

but silence is a thief,

stealing moments, stealing dreams,

stealing the chance to be seen, to be heard, to be alive.

so now, i choose to speak.

i choose to stand tall, to take up space,

to say what's in my heart,

even if my voice shakes.

because i have spent too many years whispering,

too many years waiting for permission

to be something i was always meant to be—

myself.

15. breaking point

that girl is tired.
not the kind of tired that a full night's sleep can fix,
not the kind that fades with a day off or a warm bath.
no, she's tired deep in her bones,
tired in a way that rest can't touch.
this kind of exhaustion comes from giving,
from stretching herself too thin,
from being everything for everyone,
and getting nothing in return.
she sits there, holding herself together,
masking the cracks with a practiced smile,
hiding the storm behind tired eyes.
she's been dying inside—
piece by piece, breath by breath—
and the cruelest part?
it's you who's been breaking her.
you don't see it, do you?
how she forces herself to laugh,
how she swallows her sadness
so you don't feel uncomfortable.
she's been carrying the weight of this love,
this home, this life,
while you walk free, unburdened,
never stopping to ask if she's okay.
and when you do ask,

it's not because you want the truth—
it's because you want to hear her say she's fine
so you don't have to do the work of loving her better.
she was supposed to be safe with you.
you were supposed to be her refuge,
her shelter, her peace—
but now she's just surviving
in a place that feels nothing like home.
and the worst part?
the part that cuts her the deepest?
it's you.
the one she was supposed to turn to,
the one she trusted most,
the one who should have been her softest place to land—
you're the one dragging her down.
she's tired of always bending,
of always sacrificing,
of always making excuses for why you can't show up,
why you can't love her the way she deserves.
she's tired of being expected to understand,
to be patient, to hold on,
while you take and take and take.
she's tired of fighting for a love
that never fights for her.
and now you expect her to be strong?
to carry this hurt with grace,
to swallow her pain and keep moving?
could you do it?
could you wake up every day,

pouring love into someone
who only meets you with indifference?
could you hold the weight of the world
on your shoulders,
while the one person who should be holding you
is the one pressing you down?
and then you have the audacity to ask if she's okay.
no.
she's not okay.
that girl feels alone, unseen, unheard.
she's screaming inside,
but no one is listening.
she's done.
done being taken for granted.
done begging for the bare minimum.
done waiting for the love she deserves.
she never asked for much.
not riches, not perfection,
not grand gestures or empty words—
just effort, just care, just a love that felt like home.
but now, she's done asking.
done waiting.
done hoping that one day you'll wake up
and realize what she's worth.
and you should know—
the woman sitting before you,
the one you've been taking for granted,
is not the same girl you met.
she's not the one who stays through the hurt,

who begs for love, who accepts less than she deserves.
no, she's something else now.
something stronger, something wiser,
something free.
and when she walks away,
when you watch her pack up her heart
and take back everything she poured into you,
you'll realize—
she was never meant to be broken by you.

16. we are women

where did you find the strength? they ask,
as if it's something we must search for,
hidden beneath the weight of history,
tucked away in forgotten stories,
waiting to be uncovered like buried treasure.
but strength is not something we seek—
it has always lived within us,
quietly breathing in still moments, rising in storms,
carried in the heartbeat of those before us,
passed down in the whispers of women who came before.
we do not chase it; we are it.
we are women, honey, and strength always finds us.
it finds us in the tears we wipe away when no one is watching,
in the way we love with a fierceness nothing can break,
in the way we carry the world on our backs,
yet still dance in the moonlight as if gravity doesn't exist.
we are not taught resilience—we are born into it,
molded by time, shaped by fire,
standing tall even when the world tries to bend us.
oh, how i love being a woman.
not just for the beauty they claim to admire,
not just for the way they romanticize our pain,
but for the divinity we hold within us.
for the way we build and rebuild,
for the way we love even when we are tired,

for the way we turn suffering into wisdom,

turn heartache into art,

turn silence into a roar that cannot be ignored.

we are somebody—

not just some body.

we are not just daughters, sisters, wives, or mothers—

we are women in our own right.

we are dreams forged into reality,

battles fought in silence,

the strength of every woman before us,

standing unshaken, unafraid, unbreakable.

and when they ask where your strength comes from,

when they wonder how you keep going,

how you rise, even when life tries to pull you under—

smile. stand taller.

hold your sisters' hands and remind them:

we are women, honey.

the strength has always been ours.

17. the little me

i saw her sitting there, small and quiet,
her feet barely touching the floor.
hands folded in her lap, eyes filled with questions.
she looked just like me—because she was me.
a young lady, sitting on my bed,
carrying worries far too big for her little heart.
i walked toward her, slow and careful,
afraid that if i moved too fast, she might disappear.
when i knelt beside her, she finally looked up,
her wide eyes holding something i knew too well—
fear. sadness. hope.
i reached for her hands, and she let me hold them,
her fingers small and trembling in mine.
then, in the softest voice, she asked,
"do the heartbreaks ever stop hurting?"
i sighed and shook my head.
"they hurt," i admitted, my grip tightening around hers.
"but one day, they won't break you."
her brows furrowed as she thought,
her mind racing ahead to battles she hadn't fought yet.
"and the sleepless nights?" she whispered.
"the nights when everything feels too heavy?"
i brushed a curl from her face,
my touch as gentle as the words i spoke next.
"you'll have them," i said. *"but you'll survive them too."*

she bit her lip, hesitating before asking the hardest question of all.
"do i ever learn to love myself the way i love everyone else?"
i smiled—not out of sadness, but understanding.
"it takes time," i told her. *"but yes. you will."*
she let out a small breath,
like she had been holding it forever.
and for the first time, i noticed something in her eyes—
not just curiosity. not just fear. but pride.
not in who she had become, not in the path ahead,
but in the simple fact that she had made it this far.
and as i looked at her,
really looked at her,
i realized something too—
she was proud of me.
and maybe, just maybe,
it was time i was proud of me too.

18. a heart that still hopes

she learned long ago to stay quiet, to hold her pain deep inside,
because when she cried, they called her dramatic, too much to handle, too hard to love.
so now, she swallows her feelings like bitter medicine,
forcing a smile even when her heart feels heavy,
because she still believes that silence makes her easier to keep.
she wants to say "no," to stand up for herself, to finally put her heart first,
but the fear of being abandoned wraps around her like a chain.
she remembers the way love disappeared when she stopped agreeing,
how every boundary she tried to set was met with anger,
so she learned that being quiet kept her safe, even if it left her empty.
she gives and gives until there is nothing left,
picking up pieces of everyone else while she slowly falls apart.
she listens, she helps, she loves with everything inside her,
but when she looks around, no one is there to catch her when she breaks.
and yet, she still wonders if maybe, just maybe, someone will choose her too.
she replays every conversation, every glance, every silence,
wondering if she said the wrong thing, if she should have smiled more,
if she made herself small enough to be loved.
because once, she believed that her worth was something to be measured,
that love was not given freely, but earned like a prize.

she craves a love that feels safe, where she doesn't have to beg to be
seen,

a love where she can finally be herself without fear of losing everything.

but when someone comes close, she hesitates,

because how can she accept what she was never taught to believe?

she is the woman who carries the weight of years spent unseen,

who still fights battles no one else can see,

who still searches for the love she never received.

but even with the scars, the fears, the doubts,

she still hopes.

she still hopes.

19. the invisible woman

i wake before the sun stretches its arms across the sky,
before the world stirs, before my name is even called.
my day begins before the others'—
not with the ticking of a clock, but with the sound of footsteps waiting,
waiting for me to move, to rise, to serve.
for my work has no schedule,
it stretches from the moment my eyes open until they close in exhaustion,
or maybe, until the day they close forever.
yes, i am a wife.
they call me by many names—
mom, daughter-in-law, aunt, homemaker, sometimes just mrs.
names that fit like titles, but never tell my whole story.
my life begins in the kitchen and ends there too,
surrounded by the scent of spices and the clatter of dishes,
by the heap of clothes begging to be cleaned,
by the echoes of voices calling for food, for lessons, for care.
i am a cook, a nurse, a teacher, a therapist, a caretaker,
but never just a woman, never just me.
i watch them rest when they're tired, when they're sick,
but my hands do not stop, my feet do not pause,
because no one gives me a sick leave,
because the house does not wait for me to heal.
taking a single day to rest feels like a luxury i was never meant to have.

i watch them eat the meals i make with love,
waiting, hoping, longing for a word of praise.
but silence fills the room like an empty plate,
until a mistake is made, and the silence is shattered—
not with gratitude, but complaints, with furrowed brows,
as if a single bad meal erases the thousands before it.
is it so hard to say a kind word?
don't i deserve it?
oh, i forgot—this is my duty, isn't it?
this is what i was born to do, wasn't it?
but once, i was just a girl with dreams,
with hopes that stretched beyond these walls,
with a heart that beat for more than duty.
but no one asked, and no one cared.
they all left, moving forward with their lives,
while i stood here, year after year, never once complaining,
never once asking for more.
yet, when i whispered that i, too, had dreams,
that i, too, wanted to live a life for myself,
they called me selfish.
selfish.
how strange, that the one who gave everything
was the only one who was never given anything in return.
but still, i smile.
even when my smile falters, even when the weight feels too heavy,
because this is a lifetime job, a never-ending role,
and the girl in me—the one who dreamed,
the one who believed she was meant for more—
she stays silent.

because no one is listening anyway.

20. beyond their limits

they told me to dream, to reach for the sky,
but only the dreams they had in mind.
whenever i spoke of the fire inside me,
they laughed—like my dreams were a joke.
i tried to follow their path, to be what they wanted,
but it never felt right.
their world was too small, their rules too tight,
and i was meant for more.
somewhere along the way, i lost myself,
lost everything i once held close.
their voices drowned mine,
and i started believing them.
but deep down, my dreams never faded.
no matter how hard they tried to break them,
they were still there, waiting for me
to be brave enough to chase them.
so let them laugh. let them doubt.
i won't live in the cage they built.
because dreams aren't meant to be tamed,
and i was born to fly.

21. the price of ambition

it was never an easy choice to step beyond these walls,

to leave behind the tiny hands that once clung to me so tightly,

to silence the voice in my heart that whispered, "stay."

but dreams don't die just because a woman becomes a mother,

and so, with a heavy heart, i took my first step out the door.

but the world was waiting, not with kindness, but with questions:

"oh, you left your child at home? how could you be so cold-hearted?"

"i can't imagine a day without my baby. but i guess you can."

"she's already stepping out? shouldn't she stay home and do some chores?"

"why do you even need to work? your husband earns enough, doesn't he?"

"why are you being so stubborn?"

they saw my ambition as selfishness,

as if a mother's only purpose was to give and never receive.

they spoke as if my dreams were a burden,

as if my need to be more than just a title was a mistake.

but they didn't see the nights i cried in silence,

the guilt that sat heavy in my chest,

the way i whispered, *"i'm sorry, baby,"*

every time i left for work, my heart breaking a little more.

and when my child fell sick, i didn't think twice—

i rushed back home, reports left unfinished,

because a mother's love is not measured in hours spent away,

but in the way she always returns.

back to work, the list never ends,

reports to submit, emails to send.

groceries to order, dinner to prepare,
guests coming home—she had to be there.
her husband sighed, *"you stress too much."*
"just focus at work, stop doing so much."
she forced a smile, nodded her head,
but inside, she wished the world understood instead.
she worked as hard, gave it her all,
yet he climbed fast, while she had to crawl.
the same late nights, the same sacrifice,
but her growth was slow; she paid the price.
"it's difficult," she whispered, tears in her eyes,
"i do a thousand things, yet no one realizes."
"it's difficult," he finally said, holding her hand,
"but i'll stand by you, i'll understand."
a woman's journey is not hers alone.
she can rise, but not on her own.
she carries the world, but she needs support,
to balance her dreams and her home from the heart.
because it is difficult, yes, that is true,
but with love and strength, she will push through.

22. a love that time could not take

she never asked for much, never demanded a thing.
she existed in the quiet, in the gentle moments,
in the soft rustling of her saree as she moved through the house,
in the warmth of the kitchen where meals were made
not out of obligation, but because love was her language.
she was never the loudest, never the one to seek attention,
yet she held everything together in ways no one else could.
she loved with her hands—
the way she tucked my hair behind my ear,
the way she saved the ripest mango for me,
the way she let me sit beside her,
braiding her silver-streaked hair,
as if time itself had paused for us.
she grew old as i grew up, and i never noticed it happen.
one day, she was lifting me onto her lap,
her arms strong, her skin soft and warm against my cheek.
the next, i was taller, and she was smaller,
her steps slower, her hands trembling slightly as she poured tea.
her face, once smooth, became a canvas of time,
etched with lines that spoke of love and loss,
of days spent caring, giving, never keeping anything for herself.
she seemed fragile, like a leaf that could drift away with the next breeze,
yet in her eyes, the light of love never dimmed.

she gave love to everyone, held us all close as if she knew—

as if she understood, in a way we didn't,

that time was slipping through her fingers like sand.

she waited for me, always.

i told myself there would always be more time—

another visit, another call, another chance to sit by her side.

but time is cruel, it doesn't wait,

it doesn't warn you when the last moment has come.

and just like that, she was in a hospital bed,

too weak to call my name, too tired to hold my hand.

the last thing i did for her—

the final act of love i could give—

was to pull the blanket over her feet,

a simple gesture, something she'd done for me a thousand times before.

i didn't know it would be the last time.

i didn't know that when i walked out of that room,

i would never see her again.

she left in the silence of the night, without a goodbye,

without waiting for me to tell her how much i loved her,

how much she meant to me, how much i would regret

not coming to her more often, not sitting with her longer,

not holding her hand when she needed me the most.

i remember how she loved my mother—

with a fierce devotion, hands that never stopped giving.

but i knew—deep down, i knew—

that her love for me was different, something quieter,

something that lived in the way she checked on me,

in the way she hid little things just to give them to me later,

in the way she saw my fears even when i said nothing,

in the way she answered my calls before important days,
as if her voice alone could wrap me in protection.
she loved my grandfather too,
with a love so deep and unwavering,
a love time could never erode,
a love that i will carry with me,
a reminder that love isn't in grand declarations,
but in the small, everyday things—
in waiting, in understanding, in simply being there.
and now, she's gone, but she's everywhere.
in the way i braid my hair, in how i hold onto love,
in the way i cherish those who love me.
maybe grandmothers love their grandchildren so deeply
because they see their own children in them—
a chance to love them all over again.
maybe that's why her love felt endless,
why it still lingers in the quiet moments,
why i still search for her in the spaces she used to fill.
and maybe, just maybe,
somewhere beyond the sky,
she's watching,
still loving me,
as she always did—
without hesitation,
without limits,
asking for nothing in return.

23. the daughter i always dreamed of

i used to say i never wanted kids,
told myself i was fine on my own.
no tiny hands tugging at my dress,
no soft giggles filling my home.
but somewhere deep inside my heart,
a quiet dream began to grow—
one i never dared to say out loud,
one i thought no one should know.
a little girl, my little girl,
spinning barefoot in the sun,
with ribbons tangled in her hair,
and laughter spilling as she runs.
i'd brush her hair so soft, so slow,
tie it up with little bows.
paint her nails a rosy pink,
watch her tiny fingers glow.
we'd stand in front of the mirror,
her eyes wide with so much glee.
"do i look like a princess now?"
she'd ask while smiling up at me.
and oh, how my heart would melt,
how it would ache in the best way—
because somewhere deep, i always knew,
i dreamed of her every day.

they never knew, i never said,
but this dream was always there.
to have a daughter, soft and bright,
to love, to cherish, to hold with care.
maybe i never planned this life,
maybe i thought i'd walk alone.
but now i know—without a doubt,
she was the dream i've always known.

24. more than a mother

i mothered, but i could not leave my dreams behind.

i held my child close, feeling the warmth of tiny fingers gripping mine,

but somewhere deep inside, a fire burned—

a fire i refused to let die.

i had seen it before: the quiet sacrifices,

the silent burial of dreams in the name of love.

my mother did it for me,

and her mother before her,

giving up their ambitions, their desires,

folding them away like old letters never sent.

they let go of themselves so their children could have more,

but in doing so, they lost the parts of them

that once made their hearts race,

that once made them feel alive.

i could not do that to myself.

not to my children.

i would not let them grow up

thinking that love and sacrifice meant the same thing.

i wanted to break the chain,

to be more than just a mother who gave up everything,

to be a mother who showed them how to hold on.

i wanted my children to say,

"my mother didn't quit.

neither will i."

i wanted them to see me fight,

to know that strength is not just in enduring pain
but in refusing to let the world decide your worth.
but they judged me.
they whispered behind my back,
"how can she be so cruel?
does she love herself more than her child?
why does she need to study anyway?
she'll end up in the kitchen like the rest of us.
why fight? why struggle?
isn't motherhood enough?"
but was it so wrong to want more?
was it selfish to still dream?
was i not human before i became a mother?
did my existence end the day my child took his first breath?
i studied while rocking my child to sleep,
memorized equations while stirring pots on the stove,
wrote essays in the early hours of dawn,
while the world outside rested.
i carried my future and theirs on my shoulders,
never asking for help,
never expecting applause.
because i was not just a mother.
i was a woman with dreams,
a fighter who refused to surrender,
a light for the children who would one day face their own choices.
and when they look at me,
when they see the struggle,
when they understand the fight,
i hope they say,

"my mother didn't quit.
neither will i."

25. and they called me feminist

i spoke, not to challenge, not to rebel, not to fight,

but to share the thoughts that have lived in my heart too long.

to speak of my worries, my dreams, my fears, my hopes,

to ask for things i should not have to beg for.

but the moment my voice rose above a whisper,

you frowned, you laughed, you dismissed me,

as if my words held no weight,

as if my voice didn't deserve space in this world.

i told you of the struggles i face,

the silent burdens i carry,

the battles i fight within my own home, my own mind, my own world.

i wasn't demanding, not complaining, not trying to take from you—

only trying to make you see, make you understand,

that i, too, deserve to be heard,

that i, too, have a right to be seen.

but instead of listening,

instead of trying, instead of understanding,

you gave me a name—

feminist.

you said it like it was something shameful,

like i had overstepped, like i'd spoken out of turn.

as if asking for respect meant i was demanding,

as if wanting freedom made me ungrateful,

as if voicing my pain was an act of defiance

rather than a simple plea to be acknowledged.
but tell me, did it offend you that i spoke at all?
did my voice unsettle you,
not because it was wrong,
but because it made sense?
were you afraid that if others heard me,
they might start to question,
they might start to see,
they might start to believe
that i've been right all along?
is that why you tried to silence me?
is that why you placed a label upon me,
as if a single word could erase the truth i speak?
you tell me i ask for too much,
that i should be softer, quieter, gentler.
that a good woman knows when to stay silent,
that dignity is through endurance, not through resistance.
but is it wrong to want to live with dignity,
not just endure?
is it selfish to want to walk without fear,
to speak without hesitation,
to dream without limits?
i do not ask for power over you.
i do not ask for special privilege.
i only ask for the simple right
to exist without being questioned,
to speak without being dismissed,
to be heard without being labeled.
yet my words are too much for you,

too unsettling, too honest, too real.
so you call me a feminist—
not because you truly believe i am wrong,
but because it's easier to label me
than to face the truth in my words.
and that's the part that hurts the most.
not that you called me a name,
but that you refused to listen,
that you chose to mock me
rather than understand me.
but i will not stop speaking.
not because i want to fight,
not because i want to prove a point,
but because i want to be heard,
because i deserve to be heard.
and if that makes me a feminist,
then so be it.

26. mama bear's promise

little one, walk with fire in your heart, but let it warm, not burn,
be fierce when the world tests you, but soft enough to learn.
let your voice rise like thunder when you stand for what's right,
yet carry grace like a whisper, turning storms into light.
stand tall like mountains, strong, unshaken, bold,
but cradle kindness in your hands, like treasure made of gold.
your strength lies in your spirit, your wisdom in your soul,
and the love you give to others will be what makes you whole.
the world may not always be gentle, it may push, it may shove,
but know you're wrapped in armor, woven from courage and love.
i'll be the ground beneath you, steady, firm, and wide,
and when the world feels heavy, you can always find a place to hide.
i'll shield you when you're weary, i'll roar when you feel small,
but i'll teach you when to fight and when to let things fall.
you'll know the weight of kindness, the beauty of being fair,
and if ever you should falter, look close—i'm always there.
so chase your dreams, my darling, let nothing stand in your way,
you were made for something greater, and i'll cheer you every day.
and when life feels overwhelming, when the path is dark and black,
remember this, my love—mama's always got your back.

27. love that never ends

i have known her love my whole life, fierce and unshaken,
the kind that held me when i fell, the kind that stayed when others left.
she was the voice that calmed my storms, the hands that wiped away my tears,
the heart that never wavered, no matter the passing years.
she was my safe place, my home, my guide,
the one who carried my worries, who stood always by my side.
i thought i knew every part of her, every story she had to tell,
but the day she became a grandmother, i saw something new as well.
she held my child with trembling hands, her eyes shining bright,
and in that moment, i saw her love burst into even greater light.
her voice was softer, her laughter deeper, her joy beyond compare,
as if loving my child unlocked something more rare.
i watched her trace tiny fingers, press a kiss to newborn skin,
and in that instant, i realized—i was seeing her all over again.
the same love that raised me, the same strength, the same care,
but now it stretched even further, wrapping my baby in prayers.
she sings the same lullabies, hums the same sweet tune,
whispers promises in the dark beneath the watching moon.
and when my baby cries at night, i see her standing near,
no exhaustion in her eyes—just love, just warmth, just years.
she was my mother first, the woman who shaped my way,
but now she's something more—something words can't quite say.
a grandmother, a heart grown bigger, a love that never fades,

a second chance to hold a child, to guide them through the maze.
and as i watch her love my baby, as only she can do,
i know, deep in my soul, that i was loved like this too.
for the love of a mother never dies, it only grows anew,
and in my child's heartbeat, i feel her love come through.

28. for the little girl i used to be

i saw a picture of myself today—
a little girl with bright eyes,
holding a handful of stickers she never used,
saving them for a future that never waited.
she believed she had all the time in the world,
that growing up would be magical,
that dreams would unfold like the pages of her favorite book.
she thought one day she'd open that box,
use those stickers, write letters to herself,
but that day never came.
somehow, time moved faster than she did.
it slipped through her fingers like sand,
like the childhood she never realized was leaving
until it was gone.
now, i sit here, twenty-five years old,
trapped in a body that doesn't quite feel like mine.
i still feel like i'm that fifteen-year-old,
like i was just a kid with big dreams yesterday.
i wanted to explore, to wander, to feel alive,
but instead, i spent too many days comparing,
too many nights doubting,
too many years waiting for a perfect moment
that never arrived.

and now, here i am,
watching my twenties slip away,
just like childhood did.
and i wonder—what if i blink, and again,
i'm forty, looking back,
realizing i still wasn't ready to let go?
what if life keeps moving forward
before i've had the chance to live it?
i don't want to regret again.
i don't want to keep saving the good things for later.
so now, i will buy myself flowers,
not for anyone else, just for me.
i will sit in coffee shops,
study, read, write, dream,
breathe in the warmth of a moment that is mine.
i will take myself on dates,
watch the sun rise after a morning workout,
cook dinner for myself, set the table like i deserve it.
because i do.
because we all do.
time will still move, faster than i want it to.
but this time, i won't just watch it pass.
i will live inside it,
feel every second,
embrace every version of myself—
the little girl who dreamed,
the teenager who doubted,
the woman who is still learning
that she is enough.

and i won't let life slip through my hands again.

29. the heart of an older sister

older sisters are like shadows that never leave,
always close, always watching, even when we don't see.
they act like they have better things to do,
like your chaos is just another mess they're tired of stepping through.
they sigh when you borrow their clothes,
roll their eyes when you ask for advice,
yet somehow, they always know when you need them—
and they show up without thinking twice.
they're the ones who hand over their favorite sweater,
grumbling that we'll ruin it, but still letting us wear it.
the ones who scold us when we make the wrong choice.
they teach you how to stand your ground,
how to own your mistakes instead of running away,
and sometimes, just sometimes,
how to bend the rules and not get caught at the end of the day.
they know when we're hiding pain behind a fake smile,
and when we fall apart, they sit beside us for a while.
they may not always say, *"i'm proud of you,"* out loud,
but if you listen closely, it's in the way they cheer the loudest in a crowd.
it's in the way they show up when no one else does,
in the way they hold us together when we feel like giving up.
they're part teacher, part warrior, part home,
sometimes the ones we argue with, yet always standing by our side.
and if we are lucky, before anyone else,

they become our very first best friend.
so, to the older sisters who love without saying the words,
who teach us, fight for us, and remind us of our worth—
thank you for being the steady light in our lives,
even when we don't always realize it.

30. sisters of the heart

women need women, not as rivals, but as hands to hold,
a voice in the dark whispering, *"you are bold."*
a shoulder to lean on when the world feels too tough,
a heart that whispers, *"you are enough."*
no battles of beauty, no war over grace,
no silent daggers, no whispered disgrace.
only eyes that sparkle when yours start to shine,
only hands that reach out and say, *"you are divine."*
when your spirit is weary, when your fire burns low,
i'll stoke your embers and help you glow.
i won't let envy cloud my view,
because my victories mean nothing if they don't lift you too.
we are not here to break, we are here to rise,
to wipe away each other's tears, not roll our eyes.
to celebrate victories, no matter how small,
to remind each other, *"you can have it all."*
when doubt creeps in and dims your light,
i'll be the voice that says, *"keep up the fight."*
and when you feel lost, unsure, or weak,
i'll remind you—your soul is fierce, your heart unique.
no jealousy, no hate, no whispered lies,
just open arms and unwavering ties.
a sisterhood unshaken, a bond so true,
i love you, i see you, i'm here for you.

31. the topper girl

they say, "*you'll get a good grade anyway,*"
as if the nights i spent drowning in books never happened,
as if the fear in my heart was never real,
as if success was promised to me, not something i bled for.
they don't see my hands trembling before an exam,
or the way my mind whispers, "*what if you fail?*"
they don't know how my heart burned with the fear of failure—
because i am a girl, and the world is waiting for me to fall.
they say, "*why are you so scared?*"
but they don't carry the weight i do,
they don't know what it means to prove yourself twice as hard,
to walk a road where every step is questioned,
where confidence is called arrogance,
where being great is never enough.
i do not chase love, i do not chase validation—
i chase my dreams, my ambition, my power.
and that makes them uneasy, that makes them whisper,
because a girl who knows her worth is the loudest storm.
they say, "*you never fail,*" but they don't know the truth,
they don't see the exhaustion behind my eyes,
they don't feel the weight of expectations crushing my chest,
or hear the silent prayers i whisper before every test.
i have fallen before, i have doubted, i have broken,
but i have also risen, again and again.
i have topped the class, the school, the exams,

not because i was lucky,

but because i fought for it with everything i had.

so i tell myself—

wake up, the topper inside you.

remember the girl who conquered without revisions,

who stood tall even when her hands shook,

who never let failure define her,

who always found a way.

this is just another step, just another storm—

and you were born to rise above it.

so let them talk, let them doubt, let them wait for you to fall.

and then, show them the fire they tried to put out.

32. the power of a woman who knows

they throw assignments at me like stones, hoping i'll stumble,
hoping the weight of unread pages and deadlines will make me give up,
hoping i'll sit back, accept defeat, and say, "*maybe this isn't for me.*"
but they don't know the fire i carry,
the hunger in my heart that refuses to be silenced,
the voice in my head that says, keep going, keep pushing, keep fighting,
because i am not here to surrender.
they would rather see me searching for confidence than standing in it,
would rather see me question myself, second-guess my place,
because a woman who knows her worth is a woman they cannot control.
they do not want me to realize how powerful i am,
how my mind, sharp as it is, cannot be dulled by their doubts,
how my ambition, fierce as it is, will not be tamed by their fear.
because when a woman refuses to shrink, she becomes a storm,
and storms do not ask for permission to rise.
they say, why do you study so much? why do you work so hard?
as if i should be content with being just enough,
as if i should smile and settle for less,
as if i should care more about how i look in the mirror
than how i shape my future.
but i do not have time to be pretty for their approval,

to soften my edges just to make them comfortable,

to pause my dreams so i don't intimidate the ones who dream smaller.

i have things to learn, exams to pass, a life to build—

and i refuse to fail just because they expect me to.

let them doubt me, let them whisper, let them hope i break.

let them watch as i burn brighter,

as i rise higher,

as i prove them wrong without ever needing to say a word.

because i am not here to be delicate.

i am here to be unstoppable.

33. the quiet longing of my heart

if only i could hear it once,
the words my heart has longed to know—
"you will get whatever you wanted,
happiness is yours to own."
they say the world is filled with joy,
yet why does it feel so far?
why do i stand with empty hands,
chasing dreams like falling stars?
tell me once—just once—
that i have the right to be free.
that i don't need to choose happiness,
one day, it will choose me.
if i take the step, if i try,
will the world finally see?
that i was never meant to fade,
that light was always meant for me?
please, just once—say it,
and i swear, i will believe.
"you have the right to every happiness…
just once, try to take the risk."

34. they called me selfish

they called me selfish, but they never knew,

the battles i fought, the storms i walked through.

i never asked for things my heart desired,

i stayed quiet while my dreams expired.

i became an easy child, asked for no more,

silenced my wishes, let my heart stay poor.

even the smallest things done for me,

were met with words that stung too deep.

i watched my friends with wishes so bright,

new clothes, new shoes, their future in sight.

but i counted coins, held my heart tight,

and told myself, "*it will be alright.*"

birthdays passed with no candle's glow,

no gifts to open, no ribbons to show.

but i smiled, i laughed, i played along,

hiding my pain, staying strong.

they never saw the nights i cried,

the silent prayers i kept inside.

wishing just once, i could say,

"*i want this, too*"—but i stayed away.

for every dream i let slip away,

for every wish i chose not to say,

i gave my childhood, my teenage years,

to ease their burdens, to dry their tears.

i watched my parents struggle and fight,
working so hard, day and night.
so i made a promise deep in my soul,
to never be a weight, to never take a toll.
no school trips, no movie nights,
no careless joys, no silly fights.
just a quiet child, learning to be,
a grown-up too soon, with no room to breathe.
i sacrificed my dream course, too,
the one thing i wanted, the life i once drew.
but they never asked, they never cared,
and still, their support was never there.
and yet today, they point at me,
saying, "*you're selfish, can't you see?*"
oh, if only they knew, if only they felt,
the love i carried, the life i shelved.
now when i do the smallest things for me,
guilt grows bigger, i cannot break free.
regretting the things i buy for my joy,
as if i don't deserve what others enjoy.
but i won't ask, i won't explain,
i'll bear the weight, i'll take the pain.
for those who give without a sound,
are rarely seen, are rarely found.
so call me selfish, if that's what you see,
but i know the truth that lives in me.
a heart that sacrificed, a soul that gave,
a childhood lost—so love could be saved.

35. little me would be so proud

i used to dream in colors so bright,

painting my future with fearless delight.

eyes wide, heart open, arms stretched to the sky,

believing the world was a place i could fly.

i wanted to be strong, to be kind, to be wise,

to laugh without fear, to never disguise

the fire inside me, the dreams in my chest,

to grow up and give life my very best.

and somewhere between the years that went fast,

between love and heartbreak, between first and last,

between losing myself and finding my way,

i became the person i wished for one day.

but i almost missed it—this moment so sweet,

this quiet victory, this feeling complete.

because i was too busy, too tired, too caught

in chasing what i already got.

if only i could reach back in time,

to whisper to that younger mind,

to tell her, "*look, we made it through,*

and everything you dreamed? it all came true."

she would see me now, standing tall,

not perfect, not fearless, not knowing it all,

but still, she'd smile—oh, how she'd shine—

because i became hers, and she became mine.

and in that moment, i finally see,
little me is so proud of me.

36. a woman has no home

tell me, where does a woman belong?

she is born in a house where she takes her first steps,

where she learns to laugh, to dream, to love.

she calls it home, holds it close to her heart,

but from the very beginning, she is reminded—

"this is not yours. one day, you will leave."

why does she spend her childhood

loving a place that was never meant to be hers?

why does she build memories in rooms

where she will one day be just a visitor?

why does her laughter fill the walls

of a house that will one day shut its doors on her?

then the day comes when they drape her in silk,

place gold in her hands and tears in her eyes.

her mother holds her close but still lets go,

because this is how it has always been.

"this is your new home," they tell her,

as she steps into a house full of strangers,

as she leaves behind the only place she has ever known.

is it really hers?

she tries to make it her own—

tries to fit in, tries to love,

tries to turn walls into warmth,

tries to carve a space for herself.

she gives and gives, until there is nothing left.

yet when she speaks, they silence her.
when she cries, they ignore her.
when she asks for love, they call her demanding.
and one day, when she refuses to bend,
he looks at her with cold eyes and says—
"if you don't like it, you can leave."
so where does she go?
she turns back to the house where she was born,
to the family that once called her theirs.
she stands at the door, heart in her hands,
but she is met with silence.
"you are married now," they tell her.
"you belong there."
but where? where does she belong?
the house that raised her tells her to go,
the house she married into tells her to leave.
so where is her home?
where does she rest when she is tired?
where does she cry when her heart is heavy?
where does she feel safe when the world is cruel?
she stands between two places,
one that sent her away,
one that threw her out.
and in that moment, she finally understands—
a woman has no home.
a woman gives her life to building homes,
but in the end, she has none.
she turns houses into warmth,
but has no walls to call her own.

she is the heart of a home,

but she is always an outsider.

because the moment she questions,

the moment she says no,

they remind her—she has nowhere to go.

so when will a woman have a home that is truly hers?

not one she is given, not one she is borrowed,

but one she owns, one she belongs to,

one where no one can tell her to leave.

where is a woman's home?

because all she sees are doors that close behind her.

37. she's mine, in every way that matters

did not carry her in my womb, yet she lives in my heart,
from the very first time i held her, we were never apart.
not a mother, not by birth, but in every way that counts,
she is the love i never asked for, yet i can't live without.
she holds my fingers, tiny and soft, with trust in her eyes,
and in that moment, i understand—love needs no ties.
her laughter fills the empty spaces i never knew were there,
a melody so beautiful, woven with love and care.
i am not the one who gave her life, yet she gives life to me,
with every smile, every hug, every moment she's free.
she runs to me with open arms, calling out my name,
as if i am her safe place, her warmth, her flame.
i watch her grow, i hold her close, i wipe away her tears,
i cheer her on, i calm her storms, i battle all her fears.
she may not be my daughter, not in the world's eyes,
but in my heart, she's my forever, my moon, my skies.
i tuck her in, i stroke her hair, i whisper in her ear,
"you are loved beyond the stars, i'll always be near."
not a parent, not by title, but oh, in love so deep,
she's already my child, a bond my soul will keep.
so when the world asks who she is, and why i love her so,
i'll simply smile and softly say, *"she's mine—i just know"*

38. the girl who faded away

she was the kind of girl who found joy in the little things—
the smell of rain on dry earth, the way the wind played with her hair,
the laughter of strangers that felt like music in a crowded street.
she believed in love, in kindness, in the goodness of people.
she believed that if she gave enough of herself,
the world would hold her gently in return.
but the world was not as gentle as she had hoped.
people took her kindness without giving it back,
left her waiting for words that never came,
turned their backs when she needed them most.
she learned, slowly and painfully,
that love is not always safe, and not all people stay.
she started to change, though no one really noticed.
her laughter, once so full and free, became quieter.
she stopped running barefoot in the grass,
stopped looking at the stars as if they held all the answers.
she began to sit on the edges of conversations,
afraid to speak, afraid to take up too much space,
afraid that no one really wanted her there.
she still smiled, but it was different now—
a smile that didn't quite reach her eyes,
a smile that said, i'm fine, even when she wasn't.
she still loved, but carefully, cautiously,
afraid of being too much, or worse, not enough.
she still hoped, but only in whispers,

because hope had let her down too many times before.
by the time she was twenty, she was already fading.
by forty, she had stopped looking for the life she once dreamed of.
by seventy, she had spent decades pretending she was okay.
and when they lowered her into the ground,
her best friend stood there, dry-eyed, staring at the coffin.
not because she didn't love her,
but because she had already lost her long ago.
some people don't leave when their hearts stop beating.
some are lost long before that,
drifting further away, little by little,
until one day, there is nothing left of them at all.

39. the circle of time

i remember the days when i slept till noon,
no worries, no rules—just me and my room.
you called my name, but i wouldn't reply,
too lost in my world, i don't know why.
my clothes were scattered, my bed never made,
i left things undone, i laughed, i played.
you scolded me softly, you tried to explain,
but i rolled my eyes and ignored your pain.
i thought you were strict, i thought you were wrong,
i never once saw your days were so long.
i didn't notice the love in your sighs,
or how you wiped tears from your tired eyes.
but time moves on, and now i see,
life has played the same trick on me.
now i wake up before the sun,
cooking, cleaning—work never done.
tiny hands now pull at me tight,
soft cries wake me in the middle of the night.
the same lullabies you once used to sing,
i now hum to my little one, the very same thing.
i pick up my phone, i whisper your name,
wishing you knew i feel just the same.
how did you do it, through all those years,
with so much love and hidden tears?
i hear your words in the things that i say,

i walk in your steps every single day.

the lazy child who never understood,

has now become a mother—just like she should.

time has a way of teaching us all,

time has changed me, it taught me well,

and now, mom,

i see your love, i feel your pain,

and if i could, i'd go back again.

to hug you more, to say i care,

to show you love while you were there.

but life moves forward, and so must i,

carrying your love as the years pass by.

40. the unwanted heir

"you don't need a son, my love," my mother said with kindness in her voice.
"our daughter is our light, our strength, our heir—she is the best choice.
she carries the fire of our blood, the wisdom of our past.
she is enough for both of us, her love will always last."
but my father shook his head, his eyes were cold and stern.
"a man must rule, a man must fight, a kingdom is not hers to earn.
"a daughter's hands are soft and weak, her heart too full of dreams.
she cannot wear the crown i built; she cannot lead my team."
the years went by, and war arrived, its shadow dark and wide.
the land was torn, the people feared, and father stood aside.
he waited for a son to come, a prince to take his place,
but no son was there, no warrior stood—just me with my mother's grace.
so i stepped forth with trembling hands, my heart was loud but sure.
the sword felt heavy in my grip, but my soul was even more.
through battle cries and burning lands, through pain and endless fear,
i stood where no one thought i could, and wiped away my tears.
when the war was won, the silence fell, the people knelt before me.
i looked at father's tired face, his pride now plain to see.
with tearful eyes, he took my hand, his voice was barely clear,
"forgive me, child, for now i know—you were always meant to be here."
no son was born to take the throne, no prince to wear the crown.
yet there i stood, a queen so strong, who never let them down.

the world had doubted, the world had feared, but i had proved them wrong.

for i was not just someone's child—i was a queen all along.

41. my little one

there was a time, not long ago,
when you held my hand and wouldn't let go.
you followed me close, step by step,
my voice the song that helped you rest.
you loved my hugs, my silly rhymes,
we danced in the kitchen a thousand times.
you'd run to me with open arms,
believing i could shield you from harm.
i got used to your laughter near,
your tiny whispers in my ear.
i learned your world, your every way,
and loved you more with every day.
now you've grown, and things have changed,
you see the world through wider frames.
you might find me awkward, not so cool,
and shake your head at things i do.
but i only learned to love you more,
the way i did when you were four.
no matter how tall or far you roam,
you'll always be my heart, my home.

42. i love being a mom

they ask,

"do you just love it?"

with wide eyes and soft smiles,

as if the answer should be obvious.

as if every moment is a dream,

as if i've never felt more whole,

more fulfilled,

more at peace.

and i know what i'm supposed to say.

so i do.

i smile,

nod,

say, *"yeah, i love it."*

because that's what moms say, right?

but inside—

inside, i feel the weight of words i don't say.

because yes, i love this little soul

more than i ever thought possible.

i love the warmth of tiny hands on my skin,

the way their breath slows against my chest,

the way their laughter cracks through the exhaustion

like sunlight breaking through a storm.

but i also miss myself.

i miss thinking clearly,

following a thought from start to finish

without losing it somewhere between diapers and dishes.
i miss my body—
not the way it looked, but the way it felt like mine.
i miss moving through the world freely,
without planning, without packing,
without feeling like i'm carrying the weight of a universe
in my arms.
and the anger—
oh, the anger burns in ways i don't know how to explain.
not at them, never at them,
but at the world, at myself,
at the expectations that press down on me,
telling me to be grateful,
to be happy,
to be content with this version of me
that i barely recognize.
maybe i should be.
maybe i will be.
maybe this love is supposed to stretch me
so wide, so thin,
that i forget where i end and they begin.
because despite it all,
despite the exhaustion, the loneliness, the fear—
i do love this.
i love them.
i love the way they need me,
the way their tiny fingers wrap around mine,
the way they look at me like i am their whole world.

i love them enough to lose myself,
but i also hope—
one day,
somehow,
i'll find myself again.
so i smile,
nod,
say, "*yeah, i love it.*"
and maybe,
just maybe,
one day it will feel like the whole truth.

Author's Note

Hey there,

First of all, thank you for picking up this book. It means the world to me. "SHE" is close to my heart, and I hope that somewhere in these pages, you find a piece of yourself too.

This book has been a journey; written over different phases of my life, inspired by real stories, emotions, and experiences. Some of them are mine, some belong to the incredible women around me. But most of all, this book is for you; for every woman who has ever felt unheard, unseen, or unappreciated.

I would love to hear your thoughts, reflections, and experiences after reading "SHE." If this book has resonated with you in any way, feel free to reach out to me at *faiseena.faisal5@gmail.com*. Your words mean the world to me, and I would be honored to hear your stories.

With love,

Faiseena Faisal

Acknowledgements

Though my name appears as the author of this book, "she" would not have come to life without the love, support, and presence of the incredible people who stood beside me. This book is as much theirs as it is mine.

To my sister, my most honest critic, and my biggest supporter. You saw this book take shape, page by page, you saw my excitement and fears. Your encouragement, insights, and belief in me made this book what it is today. Thank you for being a second mother to my children; without you, I wouldn't have even dared to think about publishing this book. And yes, you will forever be the coolest, most loved aunt by my kids, there is no competition!

To my children, you are my greatest blessings. You have taught me more about life and myself than I ever thought possible. You are the best. I love you endlessly. Just... try not to prove me wrong about that 'best' part, okay?

To my husband, thank you for being my anchor, my safe place, and my strength. You once told me I am a part of your rib, close to your heart; to keep me safe, to love, to hold me dearly. And that is exactly what you have done. You stood by me through thick and thin, holding my hand when I was falling apart; especially during my postpartum struggles, and reminded me that I was never alone. I couldn't have chosen a better person to be the father of my children. Me and our little ones are so lucky to have you. I am forever grateful to spend my life with you.

To my mother, you are my everything. I wouldn't be here without your love, strength, prayers, and unwavering support. I am truly grateful for all that you have endured and sacrificed for us. And I'm sorry it took me so long to realize that you, too are just a girl living her life for the first time.

To my father, you are my strength, my first friend, my guiding light. You taught me life, showed me the world, and shaped my understanding of it. For you, I will always be a hand to hold, a star that never stops shining. Thank you for being there. I love you.

With all my heart,

Faiceena Faisal